50 Delicious Chocolate Recipes for Home

By: Kelly Johnson

Table of Contents

- Classic Chocolate Cake
- Chocolate Brownies
- Chocolate Chip Cookies
- Chocolate Mousse
- Chocolate Truffles
- Chocolate Pudding
- Chocolate Lava Cake
- Chocolate Cheesecake
- Hot Chocolate
- Chocolate Ice Cream
- Chocolate Soufflé
- Chocolate Fudge
- Chocolate Ganache
- Chocolate Cupcakes
- Chocolate Tart
- Chocolate Croissants
- Chocolate Chip Banana Bread
- Chocolate Pancakes
- Chocolate Donuts
- Chocolate Milkshake
- Chocolate-Dipped Strawberries
- Chocolate Bark with Nuts
- Chocolate Caramel Bars
- Chocolate Chip Muffins
- Chocolate Eclairs
- Chocolate Chia Pudding
- Chocolate Fondue
- Chocolate Cream Pie
- Chocolate Peanut Butter Cups
- Chocolate Almond Biscotti
- Chocolate Marshmallow Fudge
- Chocolate Dipped Pretzels
- Chocolate Babka
- Dark Chocolate Raspberry Bars
- Chocolate Pecan Pie

- Chocolate Tiramisu
- Chocolate Macarons
- Chocolate-Covered Coffee Beans
- Chocolate Hazelnut Spread
- White Chocolate Blondies
- Chocolate Zucchini Bread
- Chocolate Protein Bites
- Chocolate Popcorn
- Double Chocolate Oatmeal Cookies
- Chocolate and Coconut Balls
- Chocolate Peanut Butter Smoothie
- Chocolate Churros
- Chocolate Yogurt Bark
- Triple Chocolate Brownies
- Chocolate-Dipped Oranges

Classic Chocolate Cake

Ingredients:

- 1 ¾ cups flour
- 2 cups sugar
- ¾ cup cocoa powder
- 2 tsp baking powder
- 1 tsp baking soda
- 1 cup milk
- ½ cup vegetable oil
- 2 eggs
- 2 tsp vanilla extract
- 1 cup boiling water

Instructions:

1. Preheat oven to 350°F (175°C). Grease two 9-inch cake pans.
2. Mix dry ingredients, then add milk, oil, eggs, and vanilla.
3. Stir in boiling water and mix until smooth.
4. Divide batter into pans and bake for 30-35 minutes.

Chocolate Brownies

Ingredients:

- 1 cup butter, melted
- 2 cups sugar
- 4 eggs
- 1 tsp vanilla extract
- 1 cup cocoa powder
- 1 cup flour
- ½ tsp salt
- ½ tsp baking powder

Instructions:

1. Preheat oven to 350°F (175°C). Grease a baking pan.
2. Mix butter, sugar, eggs, and vanilla.
3. Add cocoa powder, flour, salt, and baking powder.
4. Pour into the pan and bake for 25-30 minutes.

Chocolate Chip Cookies

Ingredients:

- 2 ¼ cups flour
- 1 tsp baking soda
- ½ tsp salt
- 1 cup butter, softened
- ¾ cup sugar
- ¾ cup brown sugar
- 2 eggs
- 2 tsp vanilla extract
- 2 cups chocolate chips

Instructions:

1. Preheat oven to 375°F (190°C).
2. Cream butter, sugars, eggs, and vanilla.
3. Mix in dry ingredients and fold in chocolate chips.
4. Scoop onto a baking sheet and bake for 10-12 minutes.

Chocolate Mousse

Ingredients:

- 6 oz dark chocolate, melted
- 3 eggs, separated
- 2 tbsp sugar
- 1 cup heavy cream

Instructions:

1. Beat egg yolks with sugar until pale.
2. Stir in melted chocolate.
3. Whip cream to stiff peaks and fold into chocolate mixture.
4. Beat egg whites until stiff and fold in. Chill before serving.

Chocolate Truffles

Ingredients:

- 8 oz dark chocolate, chopped
- ½ cup heavy cream
- 1 tsp vanilla extract
- Cocoa powder (for coating)

Instructions:

1. Heat cream until simmering, then pour over chocolate. Stir until smooth.
2. Mix in vanilla and chill for 2 hours.
3. Roll into balls and coat with cocoa powder.

Chocolate Pudding

Ingredients:

- 2 cups milk
- ½ cup sugar
- ¼ cup cocoa powder
- 3 tbsp cornstarch
- ¼ tsp salt
- 1 tsp vanilla extract

Instructions:

1. Heat milk in a saucepan.
2. Mix sugar, cocoa, cornstarch, and salt, then whisk into milk.
3. Cook until thickened, then remove from heat and stir in vanilla.
4. Cool before serving.

Chocolate Lava Cake

Ingredients:

- ½ cup butter
- 4 oz dark chocolate, chopped
- 2 eggs
- 2 egg yolks
- ¼ cup sugar
- 2 tbsp flour

Instructions:

1. Preheat oven to 425°F (220°C). Grease ramekins.
2. Melt butter and chocolate together.
3. Whisk eggs, yolks, and sugar until thick.
4. Fold in chocolate mixture and flour.
5. Pour into ramekins and bake for 12-14 minutes.

Chocolate Cheesecake

Ingredients:

- 1 ½ cups crushed chocolate cookies
- ¼ cup butter, melted
- 16 oz cream cheese
- ¾ cup sugar
- ½ cup cocoa powder
- 2 eggs
- 1 tsp vanilla extract
- ½ cup sour cream

Instructions:

1. Preheat oven to 325°F (160°C).
2. Mix cookie crumbs with melted butter and press into a pan.
3. Beat cream cheese, sugar, and cocoa.
4. Add eggs, vanilla, and sour cream.
5. Pour over crust and bake for 50-55 minutes.

Hot Chocolate

Ingredients:

- 2 cups milk
- ¼ cup cocoa powder
- 2 tbsp sugar
- ¼ tsp vanilla extract
- Whipped cream (optional)

Instructions:

1. Heat milk in a saucepan.
2. Whisk in cocoa and sugar until smooth.
3. Stir in vanilla and serve with whipped cream.

Chocolate Ice Cream

Ingredients:

- 2 cups heavy cream
- 1 cup whole milk
- ¾ cup sugar
- ½ cup cocoa powder
- 1 tsp vanilla extract

Instructions:

1. Whisk ingredients together until smooth.
2. Chill mixture for 2 hours.
3. Churn in an ice cream maker and freeze.

Chocolate Soufflé

Ingredients:

- 4 oz dark chocolate, melted
- 2 tbsp butter, plus extra for greasing
- 2 tbsp flour
- ½ cup milk
- 2 tbsp sugar
- 2 egg yolks
- 3 egg whites
- ¼ tsp salt

Instructions:

1. Preheat oven to 375°F (190°C). Grease ramekins.
2. Melt butter in a saucepan, whisk in flour, then add milk. Cook until thickened.
3. Stir in melted chocolate, sugar, and egg yolks.
4. Beat egg whites and salt to stiff peaks, then fold into chocolate mixture.
5. Pour into ramekins and bake for 12-15 minutes.

Chocolate Fudge

Ingredients:

- 3 cups chocolate chips
- 1 can sweetened condensed milk
- 1 tsp vanilla extract

Instructions:

1. Melt chocolate with condensed milk over low heat.
2. Stir in vanilla and pour into a lined baking dish.
3. Chill for 2 hours before slicing.

Chocolate Ganache

Ingredients:

- 8 oz dark chocolate, chopped
- 1 cup heavy cream

Instructions:

1. Heat cream until simmering, then pour over chocolate.
2. Stir until smooth and let cool before using.

Chocolate Cupcakes

Ingredients:

- 1 cup flour
- ½ cup cocoa powder
- ¾ cup sugar
- ½ tsp baking soda
- ½ tsp baking powder
- ½ cup milk
- ¼ cup vegetable oil
- 1 egg
- 1 tsp vanilla extract

Instructions:

1. Preheat oven to 350°F (175°C). Line a cupcake pan.
2. Mix dry ingredients, then add wet ingredients. Stir until smooth.
3. Pour into liners and bake for 18-20 minutes.

Chocolate Tart

Ingredients:

- 1 ½ cups crushed chocolate cookies
- ¼ cup melted butter
- 1 cup heavy cream
- 8 oz dark chocolate, chopped
- 1 tsp vanilla extract

Instructions:

1. Mix cookie crumbs with butter and press into a tart pan.
2. Heat cream, then pour over chocolate. Stir until smooth and add vanilla.
3. Pour into crust and chill until set.

Chocolate Croissants

Ingredients:

- 1 sheet puff pastry
- 4 oz chocolate, chopped
- 1 egg, beaten

Instructions:

1. Preheat oven to 375°F (190°C).
2. Cut pastry into triangles, place chocolate inside, and roll up.
3. Brush with egg and bake for 15-18 minutes.

Chocolate Chip Banana Bread

Ingredients:

- 2 cups flour
- 1 tsp baking soda
- ½ tsp salt
- ½ cup butter, melted
- ¾ cup sugar
- 2 eggs
- 3 ripe bananas, mashed
- 1 tsp vanilla extract
- ¾ cup chocolate chips

Instructions:

1. Preheat oven to 350°F (175°C).
2. Mix flour, baking soda, and salt.
3. In another bowl, mix butter, sugar, eggs, bananas, and vanilla.
4. Combine both mixtures and fold in chocolate chips.
5. Pour into a greased loaf pan and bake for 50-60 minutes.

Chocolate Pancakes

Ingredients:

- 1 cup flour
- ¼ cup cocoa powder
- 2 tbsp sugar
- 1 tsp baking powder
- ½ tsp baking soda
- 1 cup milk
- 1 egg
- 1 tbsp melted butter
- ½ cup chocolate chips

Instructions:

1. Mix dry ingredients in a bowl.
2. Add milk, egg, and butter, stirring until combined.
3. Fold in chocolate chips and cook pancakes on a greased skillet.

Chocolate Donuts

Ingredients:

- 1 cup flour
- ½ cup cocoa powder
- ½ cup sugar
- 1 tsp baking powder
- ½ tsp salt
- ½ cup milk
- 1 egg
- 2 tbsp melted butter

Instructions:

1. Preheat oven to 350°F (175°C). Grease a donut pan.
2. Mix dry ingredients, then add milk, egg, and butter.
3. Fill donut pan and bake for 12-15 minutes.

Chocolate Milkshake

Ingredients:

- 2 cups vanilla ice cream
- 1 cup milk
- ¼ cup chocolate syrup

Instructions:

1. Blend all ingredients until smooth.
2. Serve topped with whipped cream.

Chocolate-Dipped Strawberries

Ingredients:

- 1 lb fresh strawberries
- 8 oz dark chocolate, melted

Instructions:

1. Wash and dry strawberries thoroughly.
2. Dip each strawberry into melted chocolate and place on parchment paper.
3. Let set at room temperature or refrigerate until firm.

Chocolate Bark with Nuts

Ingredients:

- 12 oz dark chocolate, melted
- ½ cup almonds, chopped
- ½ cup walnuts, chopped
- ¼ tsp sea salt

Instructions:

1. Spread melted chocolate onto a parchment-lined baking sheet.
2. Sprinkle with nuts and sea salt.
3. Let cool completely, then break into pieces.

Chocolate Caramel Bars

Ingredients:

- 1 cup flour
- ½ cup butter, melted
- ¼ cup sugar
- 1 cup caramel sauce
- 1 ½ cups dark chocolate, melted

Instructions:

1. Preheat oven to 350°F (175°C). Mix flour, butter, and sugar, then press into a baking pan.
2. Bake for 15 minutes, then pour caramel sauce over the crust.
3. Pour melted chocolate over caramel and chill until firm.

Chocolate Chip Muffins

Ingredients:

- 1 ½ cups flour
- ½ cup cocoa powder
- ¾ cup sugar
- 1 tsp baking powder
- ½ tsp baking soda
- ½ cup milk
- ½ cup butter, melted
- 2 eggs
- 1 cup chocolate chips

Instructions:

1. Preheat oven to 350°F (175°C).
2. Mix dry ingredients, then add milk, butter, and eggs.
3. Fold in chocolate chips and pour batter into muffin cups.
4. Bake for 18-20 minutes.

Chocolate Eclairs

Ingredients:

- ½ cup water
- ¼ cup butter
- ½ cup flour
- 2 eggs
- 1 cup pastry cream
- 4 oz dark chocolate, melted

Instructions:

1. Preheat oven to 375°F (190°C). Boil water and butter, then add flour and stir until smooth.
2. Remove from heat, let cool slightly, then mix in eggs one at a time.
3. Pipe onto a baking sheet and bake for 25 minutes.
4. Fill with pastry cream and dip tops in melted chocolate.

Chocolate Chia Pudding

Ingredients:

- 2 cups milk
- ¼ cup chia seeds
- ¼ cup cocoa powder
- 2 tbsp honey

Instructions:

1. Mix all ingredients in a bowl.
2. Refrigerate for at least 4 hours, stirring occasionally.
3. Serve chilled.

Chocolate Fondue

Ingredients:

- 12 oz dark chocolate, chopped
- 1 cup heavy cream

Instructions:

1. Heat cream in a saucepan until simmering.
2. Pour over chocolate and stir until smooth.
3. Serve with fruits, marshmallows, or cookies for dipping.

Chocolate Cream Pie

Ingredients:

- 1 pie crust, baked
- 2 cups milk
- ½ cup sugar
- ¼ cup cocoa powder
- ¼ cup cornstarch
- 3 egg yolks
- 4 oz dark chocolate, melted
- 1 tsp vanilla extract

Instructions:

1. Heat milk, sugar, cocoa, and cornstarch over medium heat until thickened.
2. Temper egg yolks by slowly adding some hot mixture, then combine everything.
3. Stir in melted chocolate and vanilla. Pour into crust and chill.

Chocolate Peanut Butter Cups

Ingredients:

- 12 oz dark chocolate, melted
- ½ cup peanut butter
- 2 tbsp powdered sugar

Instructions:

1. Line a mini muffin tin with liners.
2. Pour a layer of melted chocolate, let set slightly, then add peanut butter mixed with sugar.
3. Top with more chocolate and refrigerate until firm.

Chocolate Almond Biscotti

Ingredients:

- 2 cups flour
- ½ cup cocoa powder
- ¾ cup sugar
- 1 tsp baking powder
- ½ cup almonds, chopped
- 2 eggs
- 1 tsp vanilla extract

Instructions:

1. Preheat oven to 350°F (175°C).
2. Mix dry ingredients, then add eggs and vanilla. Stir in almonds.
3. Shape dough into logs, bake for 25 minutes, then slice and bake for 10 more minutes.

Chocolate Marshmallow Fudge

Ingredients:

- 12 oz dark chocolate, chopped
- 1 can (14 oz) sweetened condensed milk
- 2 tbsp butter
- 1 tsp vanilla extract
- 1 ½ cups mini marshmallows

Instructions:

1. Melt chocolate, condensed milk, and butter over low heat, stirring constantly.
2. Remove from heat, stir in vanilla and marshmallows.
3. Pour into a lined pan and refrigerate until firm.

Chocolate Dipped Pretzels

Ingredients:

- 12 oz dark or milk chocolate, melted
- 2 cups pretzel rods or twists
- Sprinkles or crushed nuts (optional)

Instructions:

1. Dip pretzels halfway into melted chocolate.
2. Place on parchment paper and sprinkle with toppings if desired.
3. Let set at room temperature or refrigerate until firm.

Chocolate Babka

Ingredients:

- 3 cups flour
- ¼ cup sugar
- 1 packet yeast (2 ¼ tsp)
- ½ cup warm milk
- 2 eggs
- ½ tsp salt
- ¼ cup butter, softened
- 1 cup chocolate spread

Instructions:

1. Mix yeast, warm milk, and sugar; let sit for 10 minutes.
2. Add flour, eggs, salt, and butter, knead into a dough. Let rise for 1 hour.
3. Roll out dough, spread chocolate, roll up, and twist into a loaf.
4. Place in a loaf pan and let rise for 30 minutes.
5. Bake at 350°F (175°C) for 30–35 minutes.

Dark Chocolate Raspberry Bars

Ingredients:

- 12 oz dark chocolate, melted
- ½ cup raspberry jam
- 1 cup crushed graham crackers or cookie crumbs

Instructions:

1. Spread melted chocolate onto parchment paper.
2. Drop spoonfuls of raspberry jam and swirl with a knife.
3. Sprinkle cookie crumbs over the top. Let set before cutting into bars.

Chocolate Pecan Pie

Ingredients:

- 1 pie crust
- 1 cup pecans
- ½ cup dark chocolate chips
- 3 eggs
- 1 cup corn syrup
- ½ cup sugar
- ¼ cup melted butter
- 1 tsp vanilla

Instructions:

1. Preheat oven to 350°F (175°C). Place pecans and chocolate chips in the pie crust.
2. Whisk together eggs, syrup, sugar, butter, and vanilla. Pour over pecans.
3. Bake for 50–55 minutes. Cool before serving.

Chocolate Tiramisu

Ingredients:

- 1 cup espresso, cooled
- 2 tbsp cocoa powder
- 1 cup mascarpone cheese
- ¼ cup sugar
- 1 cup heavy cream, whipped
- 24 ladyfinger cookies
- 4 oz dark chocolate, grated

Instructions:

1. Mix mascarpone and sugar, then fold in whipped cream.
2. Dip ladyfingers in espresso and layer in a dish.
3. Spread mascarpone mixture over, then repeat layers.
4. Dust with cocoa and top with grated chocolate. Refrigerate before serving.

Chocolate Macarons

Ingredients:

- 1 cup almond flour
- 1 ¾ cups powdered sugar
- 3 tbsp cocoa powder
- 3 egg whites
- ¼ cup sugar
- ½ cup chocolate ganache (for filling)

Instructions:

1. Sift almond flour, powdered sugar, and cocoa together.
2. Whisk egg whites and sugar until stiff peaks form.
3. Fold in dry ingredients, then pipe onto a lined baking sheet.
4. Let sit for 30 minutes, then bake at 300°F (150°C) for 12–15 minutes.
5. Cool and fill with chocolate ganache.

Chocolate-Covered Coffee Beans

Ingredients:

- 1 cup roasted coffee beans
- 6 oz dark chocolate, melted

Instructions:

1. Stir coffee beans into melted chocolate.
2. Remove with a fork and place on parchment paper.
3. Let set at room temperature or refrigerate.

Chocolate Hazelnut Spread

Ingredients:

- 1 cup hazelnuts, roasted
- ½ cup powdered sugar
- 2 tbsp cocoa powder
- 2 tbsp vegetable oil
- 1 tsp vanilla

Instructions:

1. Blend hazelnuts in a food processor until smooth.
2. Add sugar, cocoa, oil, and vanilla. Blend until creamy.
3. Store in a jar at room temperature.

White Chocolate Blondies

Ingredients:

- ½ cup butter, melted
- 1 cup brown sugar
- 1 egg
- 1 tsp vanilla
- 1 cup flour
- ½ tsp baking powder
- ½ cup white chocolate chips

Instructions:

1. Preheat oven to 350°F (175°C).
2. Mix butter and sugar, then add egg and vanilla.
3. Stir in flour, baking powder, and white chocolate chips.
4. Pour into a greased pan and bake for 20–25 minutes.

Chocolate Zucchini Bread

Ingredients:

- 2 cups flour
- ½ cup cocoa powder
- 1 tsp baking soda
- ½ tsp baking powder
- ½ tsp salt
- 1 cup sugar
- ½ cup oil
- 2 eggs
- 1 tsp vanilla
- 1 ½ cups grated zucchini
- ½ cup chocolate chips

Instructions:

1. Preheat oven to 350°F (175°C). Grease a loaf pan.
2. Mix flour, cocoa, baking soda, baking powder, and salt.
3. In another bowl, whisk sugar, oil, eggs, and vanilla.
4. Stir in zucchini and dry ingredients. Fold in chocolate chips.
5. Pour into the pan and bake for 50–55 minutes.

Chocolate Protein Bites

Ingredients:

- 1 cup oats
- ½ cup peanut butter
- ¼ cup honey
- 2 tbsp cocoa powder
- ¼ cup chocolate chips
- 1 scoop chocolate protein powder

Instructions:

1. Mix all ingredients in a bowl.
2. Roll into small balls and refrigerate for 30 minutes before serving.

Chocolate Popcorn

Ingredients:

- 8 cups popped popcorn
- ½ cup dark chocolate, melted
- ¼ tsp sea salt

Instructions:

1. Drizzle melted chocolate over popcorn.
2. Toss and spread on parchment paper.
3. Sprinkle with salt and let set before serving.

Double Chocolate Oatmeal Cookies

Ingredients:

- 1 cup flour
- 1 cup oats
- ½ cup cocoa powder
- ½ tsp baking soda
- ½ cup butter, softened
- ½ cup brown sugar
- 1 egg
- 1 tsp vanilla
- ½ cup chocolate chips

Instructions:

1. Preheat oven to 350°F (175°C).
2. Cream butter and sugar, then add egg and vanilla.
3. Mix in dry ingredients, then fold in chocolate chips.
4. Drop spoonfuls onto a baking sheet and bake for 10–12 minutes.

Chocolate and Coconut Balls

Ingredients:

- 1 cup shredded coconut
- ½ cup condensed milk
- 1 cup dark chocolate, melted

Instructions:

1. Mix coconut and condensed milk.
2. Roll into balls and freeze for 15 minutes.
3. Dip in melted chocolate and let set.

Chocolate Peanut Butter Smoothie

Ingredients:

- 1 banana
- 1 cup milk
- 1 tbsp cocoa powder
- 1 tbsp peanut butter
- ½ tsp vanilla
- ½ cup ice

Instructions:

1. Blend all ingredients until smooth.
2. Serve immediately.

Chocolate Churros

Ingredients:

- 1 cup water
- 2 tbsp sugar
- 2 tbsp butter
- 1 cup flour
- 1 egg
- ½ tsp cinnamon
- ½ cup chocolate, melted

Instructions:

1. Heat water, sugar, and butter in a saucepan.
2. Stir in flour and mix until a dough forms.
3. Let cool, then add egg and mix.
4. Pipe dough into hot oil and fry until golden.
5. Dip in melted chocolate before serving.

Chocolate Yogurt Bark

Ingredients:

- 1 cup Greek yogurt
- 2 tbsp cocoa powder
- 2 tbsp honey
- ¼ cup chocolate chips

Instructions:

1. Mix yogurt, cocoa, and honey.
2. Spread on a lined tray and sprinkle with chocolate chips.
3. Freeze for 2 hours, then break into pieces.

Triple Chocolate Brownies

Ingredients:

- 1 cup butter, melted
- 1 cup sugar
- 2 eggs
- 1 tsp vanilla
- ½ cup cocoa powder
- 1 cup flour
- ½ cup dark chocolate chips
- ½ cup white chocolate chips

Instructions:

1. Preheat oven to 350°F (175°C).
2. Mix butter, sugar, eggs, and vanilla.
3. Stir in cocoa, flour, and chocolate chips.
4. Pour into a pan and bake for 25–30 minutes.

Chocolate-Dipped Oranges

Ingredients:

- 2 oranges, peeled and segmented
- ½ cup dark chocolate, melted

Instructions:

1. Dip each orange segment halfway into melted chocolate.
2. Place on parchment paper and let set.

www.ingramcontent.com/pod-product-compliance
Lightning Source LLC
LaVergne TN
LVHW081335060526
838201LV00055B/2661